What Is a GOVERNMENT?

By Jennie Thompson,
Simon Adams
and Logan Everett

Series Literacy Consultant
Dr Ros Fisher

Pearson Education Limited
Edinburgh Gate
Harlow
Essex CM20 2JE
England

www.longman.co.uk

ISBN 0 582 84131 3

Colour reproduction by Colourscan, Singapore
Printed and bound in China by Leo Paper Products Ltd.

The Publisher's policy is to use paper manufactured from sustainable forests.

The following people from **DK** have
contributed to the development of this product:
Art Director Rachael Foster

Martin Wilson **Managing Art Editor**	**Managing Editor** Marie Greenwood
Kath Northam **Design**	**Editorial** Marian Broderick
Sarah Duncan, Pernilla Pearce **Picture Research**	**Production** Gordana Simakovic
Richard Czapnik, Andy Smith **Cover Design**	**DTP** David McDonald

Dorling Kindersley would like to thank: Sarah Crouch for preliminary design work; Lucy Heaver for editorial research; Mariana Sonnenberg and Carlo Ortu for additional picture research; Johnny Pau for additional cover design work; and Hannah Wilson.

Picture Credits: Alamy Images: Brian Lawrence/Imagestate 1cla; Pictor International/Imagestate 18b; Robert Llewellyn 3. The Art Archive: Museo Provinciale Sigismondo Castromediano Lecce 12br.Bridgeman Art Library, London/New York: Museum Archeologico Nazionale, Naples. Italy 13tl. Corbis: 27tr; Ali Meyer 14tr; Paul Almasy 10tr; Archivio Iconografico S.A 15cr; Baldev/Sygma 24br; Bettmann 12cr, 15bc, 19br, 27br; Dean Conger 6br; Richard Cummins 24tr; Laura Dwight 28tl; Kevin Fleming 6crb; Tim Graham 18tr; Jose Fuste Raga 1bc; Liz Gilbert 9cr; S. P. Gillette 8bl; George Hall 9tr; Roger de la Harpe/Gallo Images 1tcl; John Van Hasslet 15tr; Langevin Jacques 29br; Jufri Kemal 23cr; Gary D. Landsman 7br; London Aerial Photo Library 8tr; William Manning 1cra; Stephanie Maze 17crb; Jose Luis Pelaez, Inc. 7cr; Roger Ressmeyer 11; Carmen Rodondo 13b; Uwe Schmid 1cb; Ferdaus Shamin 25bl; Joseph Sohm 17tr; Paul A. Souders 1cr, 17bl; Tom Stewart 8cl; David Turnley 19tr, 24bc; Peter Turnley 17c, 17br, 26b; William Whitehurst 6tl. Ecoscene: Paul Kennedy 9bl. Friedrich-schiller-universität Jena/Hilprecht Collection Of Near Eastern Antiquities: 10br. Getty Images: AFP 20cl; Paula Bronstein 25bc; Carlo Ferraro/AFP 29tr. Lonely Planet Images: Izzet Keribar 12crb. Alexander Turnbull Library, National Library Of New Zealand, Te Puna Matauranga o Aotearoa: 22br. Reuters: Mark Baker 18cl; Raheb Homavandi 20bc. Rex Features: Robert Service 32br; Tim Rooke 21c; Sipa Press 23br. Jacket: Alamy Images: Dallas and John Heaton front t. Corbis: Ludovic Maisant front cr. Getty Images: Carlo Ferraro/AFP front cl; Andrea Pistolesi back. Reuters: front bl.

All other images: DK Dorling Kindersley © 2004. For further information see www.dkimages.com
Dorling Kindersley Ltd., 80 Strand, London WC2R 0RL

Contents

What is a Government?

This book is about how different governments work. A government is the name given to the group of people who organize the way a country is run.

Governments organize a money system so people can buy and sell goods.

Governments organize transport systems so people can travel around the country.

Governments pass laws to help protect the planet and its natural resources.

Governments pass laws that the **community** or **nation** have to obey.

Governments tell the army to defend the country from attack.

Agriculture and industry are regulated (checked) by the government to keep people safe.

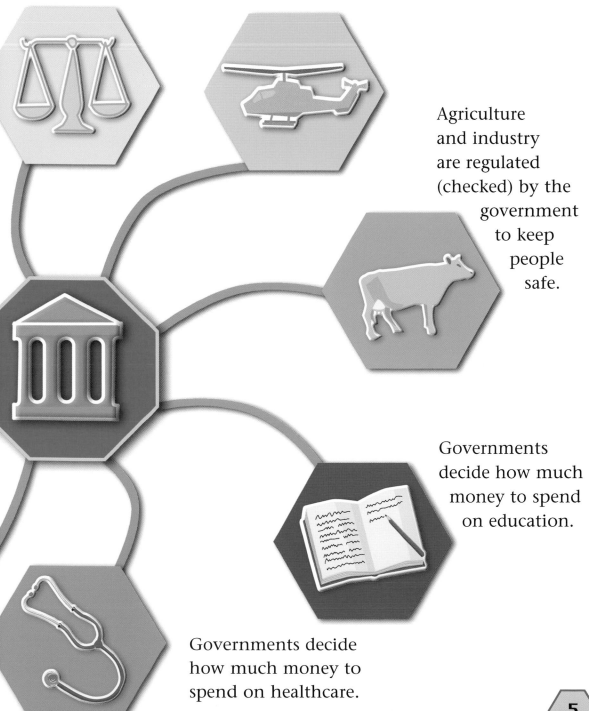

Governments decide how much money to spend on education.

Governments decide how much money to spend on healthcare.

Money Systems

Governments organize a money system so people can buy and sell goods. Money systems, or currency, vary from country to country. In Britain the currency used is pounds. In some European countries, including Ireland, France, Germany and Italy, the currency used is the Euro. Paper money and coins are produced, or minted, by the government.

banknotes and coins from around the world

Education

Governments provide schools, libraries, sports centres, art galleries and computer centres to help educate people. They pay teachers and learning support assistants to educate children in school. They pay caretakers and cleaners to take care of the buildings so they are clean and tidy. They also give schools money to buy equipment like books, computers, pens, pencils and rulers.

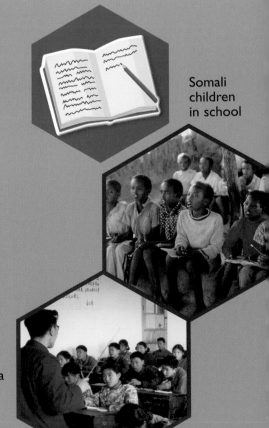

Somali children in school

children in school in China

Laws

Governments make, develop and pass laws. 'Statute Law' is the most important part of the United Kingdom's **constitution**. These are the laws that have been passed by **parliament**. In the United Kingdom **politicians** meet in the **Houses of Parliament** to decide laws and make decisions for the country. The Houses of Parliament are in the Palace of Westminster in London.

a judge in the United States

Healthcare

Governments provide healthcare for the people to make sure they stay fit and healthy. In the United Kingdom the National Health Service is available to all its **citizens**. The government pays the National Health Service to build hospitals. If you are sick the health service will provide a doctor, medicine and any equipment required to make you well again.

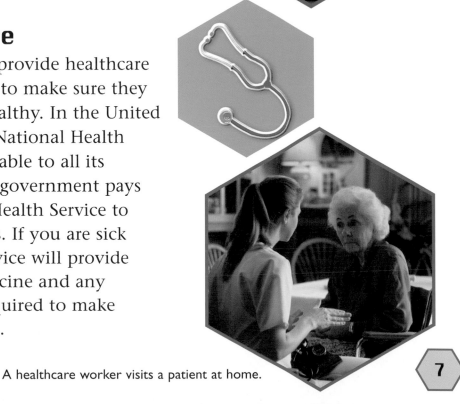

A healthcare worker visits a patient at home.

Transport Systems

People need transport for both work and pleasure. Many governments provide transport systems, such as roads, railways, ports and airports. In some countries these are run by private companies. Governments also make sure that the cars, buses, trains, boats and planes in use are safe to travel in.

Spaghetti Junction in Birmingham

sheep farm in the United States

Agriculture and Industry

Governments provide farmers with money to help them protect the land they farm. They work with them to develop new crops and better methods of farming. Governments help with the export of food and animals to other markets. They also make sure that all food is safe to eat and all farm animals are healthy.

tea harvest in India

Military Forces

A government pays for an army, navy and air force for its country. It trains men and women to serve in these military forces. These forces protect their country from invasion. They can also help other countries in need, too. Sometimes the military forces get involved in local problems. For example, when the UK's fire service went on strike in 2002 the army provided an emergency back-up service.

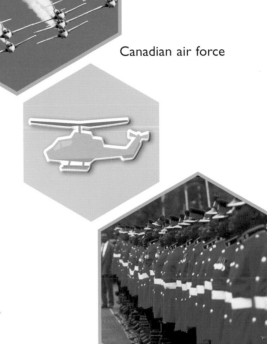
Canadian air force

Kenyan army inspection

wind farm in New Zealand

Environmental Policy

Governments help the environment by encouraging people to recycle paper, plastic and glass. They provide collection services and special banks to dispose of these items. They also help prevent pollution and protect rivers, streams and lakes from suffering from too much damage.

Early Governments

We have governments because people living together need a way to organize their lives. Over the years countries have developed different languages and **cultures** to suit the way they live. Consequently they have developed different types of governments too.

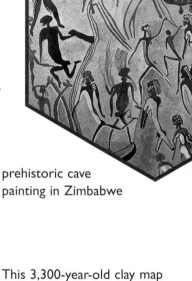

prehistoric cave painting in Zimbabwe

How Did Governments Begin?

For thousands of years people lived in small groups with their families and relatives. These groups moved around and hunted together. They didn't have governments like we do today. Instead they would discuss problems. There might have been a leader who took control in times of danger, but most decisions would have been made by the whole group.

This 3,300-year-old clay map of an ancient Mesopotamian city (in present-day Iraq) shows irrigation systems, roads and public buildings. This city must have had a government to organize these works.

Eventually some families settled in one area, and were joined by other families. They shared resources and formed into early **settlements**. New problems developed, but they couldn't be discussed with everyone. Consequently, small groups of leaders were chosen to discuss them.

As the **community** grew, so did the responsibilities of the community leaders. They discussed ways the community could share important resources like water. They talked about ways to build irrigation systems to water the crops. They discussed ways to build roads around the settlement. They tried to help the whole community work together.

Finally community leaders were replaced by different types of government. Some governments were run by one leader, and others by a group of leaders. These leaders made laws for the community.

Ancient Egypt

For centuries the people of ancient Egypt were ruled by dynasties, or families, of rulers known as pharaohs. When one pharaoh died, his or her son, brother, wife or daughter became the next ruler. Ancient Egyptians believed that the pharaohs were divine, or gods. Pharaohs lived in great luxury while many of the people lived in great poverty. Pharaohs built pyramids for their final resting places.

Pharaoh Khufu (2551–2528 BC) used local workers and slaves to build the Great Pyramid (centre).

Ancient Greece

Ancient Greece was made up of many small cities such as Athens, Sparta and Thebes. There was no single ruler. Instead each city had its own system of government.

Later a new type of government developed in Athens. It was called **democracy**, which means 'people rule'. All **citizens** voted for their leaders and took part in making decisions. However, only adult males whose parents were both from Athens could be citizens. No woman could be a citizen, even if both her parents were from Athens. Neither could slaves or foreigners be citizens. This type of democracy meant that only certain people could rule.

Pericles was a champion of democracy in ancient Greece. He built the Parthenon, a famous temple.

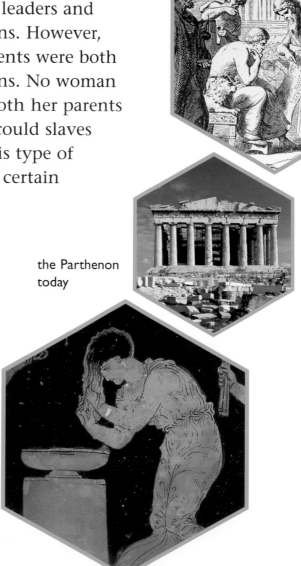

the Parthenon today

a rich woman shown washing on a 4th-century-BC vase

Ancient Rome

Legend has it that Rome was founded in 753 BC. At first Rome was a **monarchy** governed by kings. Many kings were cruel and unjust. Then in 509 BC the monarchy was overthrown and Rome became a **republic**. Two leaders ran the republic. One was a member of the upper class and the other was a member of the working class.

The Roman republic lasted until 27 BC when one leader, called Augustus, seized power and became the first Roman emperor. He had total power over every citizen in the Roman empire, which stretched across most of Europe and North Africa. All Roman emperors took advice from the Senate, which was the main law-making institution in Rome.

Claudius was a strong emperor who ruled from AD 41–54.

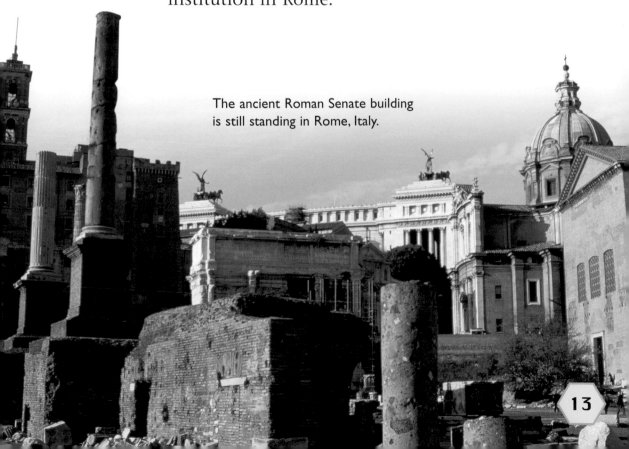

The ancient Roman Senate building is still standing in Rome, Italy.

Rulers Around the World

Ancient Egypt was ruled by pharaohs who thought they were gods, while ancient Greece was governed by its own **citizens**. Historically, however, most countries have followed ancient Rome and have been ruled by monarchs.

Between 1300 and 1922 there was an empire based in eastern Europe and western Asia known as the Ottoman empire. At the start of the empire, when an Ottoman sultan died, his sons had to fight each other before one could take control of the empire. Then the victorious son killed the others. This system of rule continued until 1603 when the eldest son automatically succeeded his father.

Japan has the oldest **monarchy**, which dates back 2,600 years. The first emperor was believed to be a direct descendant of the Sun goddess. All Japanese emperors were believed to be gods, but the real power belonged to the military rulers called **shoguns**.

Sulayman I ruled the Ottoman empire from 1520–1566. He had complete power, but was a fair ruler.

Emperor Akihito (middle) is the current emperor of Japan.

During the 1400s the Incas lived in Peru in South America. They believed that their rulers were descended from the Sun. Inca emperors sent their most powerful nobles to govern distant parts of their empire on their behalf. This way they could control their huge empire.

Pachacutec was a military hero who expanded the Inca Empire. He was made ruler in 1438.

In England monarchs ruled for hundreds of years, but they were usually men. However, one of the most famous English monarchs was Elizabeth I. She ruled from 1558–1603. She was one of the strongest and most influential rulers England has ever had.

From 1547 Russia was ruled by tsars. They had complete power and were known for their ruthlessness and ambition. Ivan IV became known as Ivan the Terrible because he killed so many people.

Elizabeth I of England

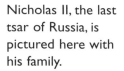

Nicholas II, the last tsar of Russia, is pictured here with his family.

Modern Types of Government

Today there are even more types of government in the world. The most common type is **democracy**. Here is a chart of the main types of government:

Type	Description	Examples
Democracy		
Parliamentary Democracy	**Elected** representatives sit in **parliament** and form a government. Includes parliamentary **republics** and constitutional **monarchies**.	Australia, Canada, Germany, New Zealand, Republic of Ireland, Spain, United Kingdom
Presidential Republic	**Citizens** directly or indirectly elect a national leader called a **president**.	Brazil, France, Russia, South Africa, United States
Alternative Forms of Government		
Communist State	Property and business is owned by the government.	Cuba, People's Republic of China
Theocracy	Power is held by religious leaders.	Iran, Vatican City
Monarchy	Power is held by the ruling monarch.	Brunei, Jordan, Oman, Saudi Arabia
Military Government	Power is seized and held by military leaders.	Myanmar (Burma), Pakistan
Dictatorship	A country ruled by a leader with absolute, or total, power.	Libya

Democracy

Most countries in the world are democracies. Usually from the age of eighteen, citizens can elect the people who will form the government. Then the government makes decisions on behalf of the citizens. Each country has developed its own style of democracy. However, there are two main types: parliamentary democracies and presidential republics.

US Declaration of Independence

In 1994 Nelson Mandela became the first democratically elected president of South Africa.

In 1984 voters celebrated the first democratic **elections** in Brazil for twenty-five years.

A man distributes election material for a **candidate**.

Albanian graffiti calling for democracy in 1992.

17

Parliamentary Democracy

Many countries in the world are parliamentary **democracies**. The United Kingdom is a parliamentary democracy because it has a government that is answerable to **parliament**. **Politicians** meet in the **Houses of Parliament** to decide laws and make decisions for the country.

Elizabeth II (middle) is the Queen of the United Kingdom.

There are two parts to parliament. First there is the House of Commons. Its members are called MPs (Members of Parliament) and are **elected** by the people in each **constituency**. Second is the House of Lords whose members are not elected. They come from different backgrounds.

In a parliamentary democracy, the head of state is not involved in party politics. In the United Kingdom the head of state is the monarch, but in some countries it is an elected **president**.

John Howard is the Australian **Prime Minister**.

The parliament building in Budapest in Hungary was built in the 19th century.

Presidential Republic

In a presidential **republic** the head of state, or president, has real power. Usually the president is elected by the people, as he or she is in Brazil, France, Russia and the United States. However, in South Africa the president is elected by parliament. In all cases the president serves for a fixed term before he or she has to be elected again or replaced. Usually the term is four to six years.

A president runs the government of a country. He or she can propose laws and also makes sure that all the laws of the country are enforced. However, laws have to be debated and approved by parliament before they come into force. Sometimes the president may appoint a prime minister to help. This is the case in France.

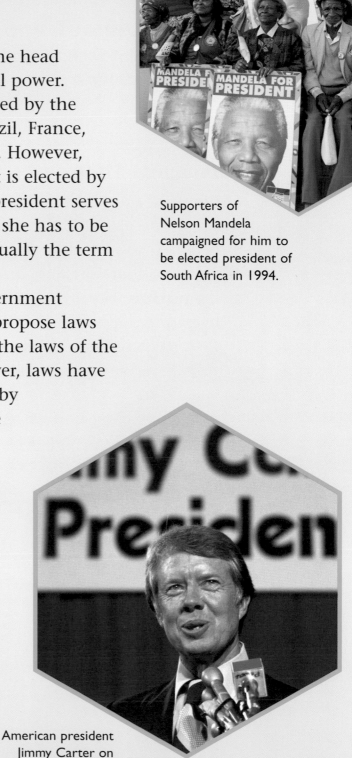

Supporters of Nelson Mandela campaigned for him to be elected president of South Africa in 1994.

American president Jimmy Carter on **election** night, 1976

Alternative Forms of Government

There are many different ways to run a country.
Here are five alternative types of government:

Communist State

Communist states like China and Cuba are based on the idea that the country itself, not individuals, should own property, industry and business, so that everyone has an equal share of the **nation**'s wealth. As everyone is equal, everyone can be represented by one party (the communist party) which runs the country on their behalf.

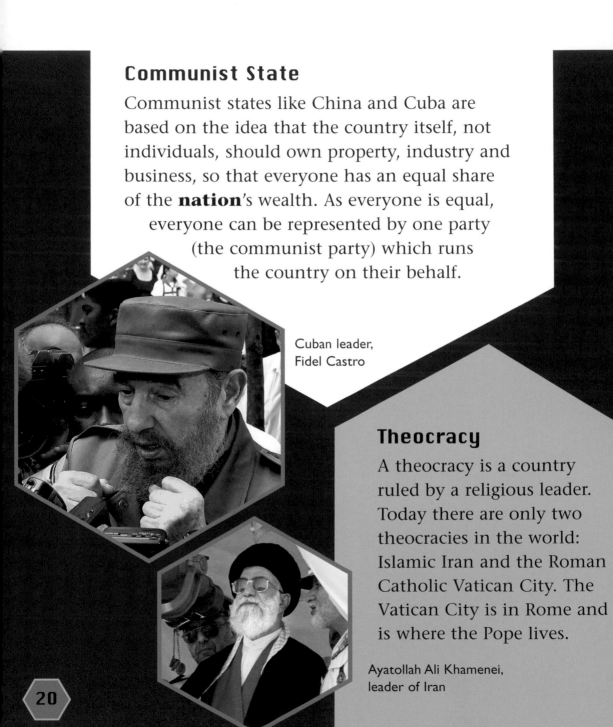

Cuban leader,
Fidel Castro

Theocracy

A theocracy is a country ruled by a religious leader. Today there are only two theocracies in the world: Islamic Iran and the Roman Catholic Vatican City. The Vatican City is in Rome and is where the Pope lives.

Ayatollah Ali Khamenei,
leader of Iran

Monarchy

A **monarchy** has a king, queen, emperor or empress as a leader. He or she is usually born into the ruling family and inherits the position. In a traditional monarchy the king or queen rules the country, as in Brunei. In a constitutional monarchy the democratic government limits the monarch's power. This is the case in the United Kingdom.

Sultan of Brunei

Dictatorship

If a country is ruled by one leader who has not been **elected** and is not a monarch then it is called a dictatorship. Dictators may have advisors to rely on but they will make the final decisions themselves. They do not usually allow **political parties**, so no one can oppose them. Dictators control the country's military services, schools, televisions and newspapers. This way the people learn only what is acceptable to the dictator.

Military Government

When a leader fails to govern properly, the military forces may intervene to run the country themselves. Although military leaders are very good at keeping law and order, they tend not to be very good at running the country. Many military rulers eventually hand over their power to an elected government.

Burmese army on parade

21

How Governments Are Chosen

A government comes into power in different ways. In the United Kingdom a government is chosen at a **general election**. First people across the whole country vote for the **candidate** who they want to represent them in **parliament**. Next the votes are counted and the candidate with most votes is **elected** as Member of Parliament. The people elected to parliament are all members of different **political parties**. The leader of the party with most members in parliament becomes **prime minister**.

When a government is run by a non-democratic ruler, such as a monarch, it changes when the monarch dies and his or her successor takes over. With a military government, the leader changes when one military leader replaces another. In both cases, the people of the country have no choice as to what their new government will be like.

Female Suffrage

Until about 100 years ago, suffrage, or the right to vote, was limited to men – and only wealthy men. No women could vote, as they were not considered equal to men. This that changed in 1869 when women in the US state of Wyoming gained the vote. In 1893, New Zealand became the first country to have universal suffrage. All women in the United States gained the vote for the first time in 1920. British women did not get equal voting rights with men until 1928.

Kate Sheppard (1847–1934), a New Zealand suffragette

Elections

Most modern governments have **elections**. In democratic elections there are usually two or more political parties. In the United Kingdom the country is split into **constituencies**. In each constituency political parties select a candidate to stand for election. The people in each constituency vote for the candidate of their choice, but only one candidate in each constituency can win. Nowadays all adult **citizens** have the right to vote. This is called universal suffrage. In the past, some countries, including the United Kingdom, have only let certain groups of people vote. Women were not allowed to vote at all until 1918 and then only if they were thirty or over. It took until 1928 for women to get the same voting rights as men.

These citizens in Jakarta, Indonesia, supported Megawati Sukarnoputri in the presidential elections.

Silvio Berlusconi celebrated becoming leader of Italy in 2001.

Candidates need to get enough votes to be **elected**. Therefore they **campaign** to tell people how they will use their power if they win. They make speeches and visit different places to meet voters.

Posters are a popular way of trying to win votes.

Voting

On **election** day every voter has the chance to vote. Some people send in their vote by post, but most go to their local polling station to vote. When the **citizens** have voted, the votes are counted. There are different ways of counting votes. In some **democracies**, like the United Kingdom, the candidate in each area with the most votes is the winner. This is sometimes called 'first past the post voting'.

An electronic voting system was used in India in 1999.

This man is voting in the South African elections in 1994.

Other democracies use a method of voting called proportional representation. For example, if a party gets 40 per cent of the votes they get approximately 40 per cent of the seats in **parliament**. Sometimes countries hold elections that are not democratic. This could happen if there was only one candidate or one **political party** to vote for. Alternatively, if votes were counted incorrectly or some of the votes were lost, then this could make the election unfair, too.

In some countries, such as the United States, people vote for the **president** and the members of parliament separately. This means that the president may be from a different political party to most of the members of parliament.

How Often Do Leaders Change?

Democracies hold elections at different intervals. Most countries have elections every two to six years, with the gap between each election either fixed or set at a maximum time. In the United Kingdom, an election for parliament must happen at least every five years. In the United States, the President is elected for four years and may be elected a second time.

Braille ballots make voting easier for blind voters.

Citizens in East Timor voted in the country's first independent elections in 1999.

How Do Governments Change?

Governments have changed and adapted to meet the needs of their **communities** since they first began. Many **nations** have **constitutions** that describe how the government can be changed and even how to change the constitution. **Elections** give voters the chance to change the **political party** in charge of the government. Governments can hold referendums. A referendum is when the **citizens** are asked to vote on one single political question. Referendums are only used occasionally by countries for very important issues. As a result of a referendum in 1975 the United Kingdom voted to stay part of the European Union.

East German patrol guards looking at West Germans demonstrating in Berlin, 1989

Governments can change as countries join together or separate. In 1945, at the end of World War II, Germany was divided into two separate countries. West Germany had one government and East Germany had another very different government. In 1990 the countries united again to form one government.

Mexican revolutionaries posing with guns drawn in 1916

Sometimes government change comes about after a revolution. A revolution is when a government is overthrown, usually by force. In 1910 poor people overthrew the government in Mexico. However, it took until 1917 for a lasting government to be set up.

One of the most important revolutions in world history occurred in Russia in 1917. People were starving to death while the **monarchy** lived in luxury. The tsar was overthrown. This eventually led to the formation of the first communist government.

Communists in Moscow, Russia, during the revolution in 1917

What's Your Role?

Writing letters to your political representative is one way of making your voice heard.

British **Prime Minister** Tony Blair meets an association for disabled schoolchildren.

Everybody in a **democracy** has the right to play a role in government, even if they cannot vote, and that includes you! You can make your voice heard, whether you agree with the government or not, in many different ways.

You can let the government know your opinions by writing letters to your **elected** leaders or to the newspapers. If you want to talk to more people you can try to get interviewed by a radio or television station. You can also go to your local leaders and explain your feelings.

When you are old enough, you may want to run for a political position and have your say directly. In the meantime, you can practise being politically active by joining school committees or participating in school **elections**.

You might feel very strongly about an issue. You could get together with others to petition, or ask for, a change to a law or ask the government to change a particular policy. The more people you get to sign the petition, the more likely the government will be to listen to your point of view.

By taking advantage of your democratic right to vote, to protest and to make your opinions known peacefully, you can help improve your government and improve the future of your town, local **community** or country.

In 2003 Italian demonstrators held a rally to protest against war in Iraq.

In 1998 Indonesian students staged a peaceful occupation of **parliament** and demanded the resignation of **President** Suharto.

Glossary

campaign   to take part in an organized series of activities in order to achieve a goal

candidate   a person who is trying to get elected to a public position such as an MP

citizen   member of a country

community   people living in one place or country, often having common interests

constituency   an area that is represented by a Member of Parliament who has been elected by its voters

constitution   the basic laws and rules that explain how a government is organized and run

culture   the customs, beliefs and values of a group of people

democracy   a system of government in which citizens take part in the decision-making process

elect   to chose by a vote

election   the process of choosing someone by a vote

general election   an election of Members of Parliament for the whole country

Houses of Parliament	the parliament of the United Kingdom, consisting of the House of Commons and the House of Lords
monarchy	a country headed by a king, queen, tsar or sultan
nation	a large community of people who live in the same part of the world under one government
political party	a political group organized on a local or national basis to put forward its views on policies and candidates
parliament	an assembly that makes the laws of a country
politician	a person who is involved in politics, especially the holder of an elected position
president	the head of state and elected leader of a republic
prime minister	the chief minister in a government
republic	a country headed by an elected leader who is not a monarch
settlements	places where people establish communities
shoguns	military commanders in Japanese history

Index